Contents

Shakespeare

Brandon Robshaw and Rochelle Scholar

Published in association with The Basic Skills Agency

Hodder & Stoughton

A MEMBER OF THE HODDER HEADLINE GROUP

Acknowledgements

Cover: Portrait of Shakespeare by Hader after Chandos (Photo AKG).
Illustrations: Mike Bell.

Orders: please contact Bookpoint Ltd, 39 Milton Park, Abingdon, Oxon OX14 4TD. Telephone: (44) 01235 400414, Fax: (44) 01235 400454. Lines are open from 9.00–6.00, Monday to Saturday, with a 24 hour message answering service. Email address: orders@bookpoint.co.uk

British Library Cataloguing in Publication Data
A catalogue record for this title is available from The British Library

ISBN 0 340 74271 2

First published 1999
Impression number   10 9 8 7 6 5 4 3 2 1
Year   2004 2003 2002 2001 2000 1999

Copyright © 1999 Brandon Robshaw and Rochelle Scholar

Typeset by Fakenham Photosetting Ltd, Fakenham, Norfolk.
Printed in Great Britain for Hodder & Stoughton Educational, a division of Hodder Headline Plc, 338 Euston Road, London NW1 3BH by Redwood Books, Trowbridge, Wiltshire.

1 London

London, 1587.

Will Shakespeare gazed in wonder.
He had never seen anything like it.

Everywhere was crowded and noisy.
Traders called out,
selling their wares.
Children ran barefoot in the streets.
Ladies in fine robes of red,
blue and green
and gentlemen with swords
at their sides
rode by.

Will looked down.
He saw rats running along the gutters.
The streets were narrow and dirty.
People threw filth and rubbish
out of the windows.

Will looked up.
He saw the spires of churches
glinting in the sun.
Tall ships with white sails
sailed up the River Thames.
London Bridge was crowded
with shops and houses.
Heads of criminals
were stuck on top of the bridge gates.

Will Shakespeare was 23 years old.
He came from the town
of Stratford-upon-Avon.
Stratford was a small town –
about 1,500 people lived there.

London was very different.
100,000 people lived there.
It was full of life and excitement.

Will decided he liked it.
He decided to stay.

2 Early Days

William Shakespeare was born
on 23 April 1564.
His father was a glovemaker.
His mother, Mary Arden,
had some land and money of her own.
They weren't rich,
but they were quite comfortable.

Stratford was a small market town,
surrounded by green fields.
Will was sent
to Stratford Grammar School
when he was seven.
He had to learn Latin there.
The school day was 11 hours long
and he had to go six days a week.

Will hated it.
A long time later, in one of his plays,
he wrote of a schoolboy
'creeping like snail
unwillingly to school'.

When Will was 12,
his father got into debt.
The glove business
was not doing well.
He could no longer afford
to keep Will at school.

Will was taken from school
and went to work for his father,
making gloves.
That was all the education Will had.

When Will was 18, he got married
to Ann Hathaway.
She was the daughter of a local farmer.
She was eight years older than him.
They probably had to get married
because she was pregnant.
The baby, Susanna,
was born six months after the wedding.

Two years later, Ann gave birth to twins.
They were called Judith and Hamnet.

Not long after this,
Will left Stratford and went to London.
No one really knows why.
One story is that he was caught
poaching deer,
and had to run away to London
to escape prison.

He stayed in London
for the next 23 years.
He sent money home to his family
and visited them about once a year.

3 The Theatre

When Will first arrived in London,
he had no money and no job.
He earned his living
by holding people's horses
when they went to the theatre.

People from all walks of life
went to the theatre.
The rich sat in the balcony.
Poorer people paid a penny
to stand near the stage.
Food and drink were on sale.
It was a much livelier, noisier place
than the theatre of today.

The plays were full of action.
There were love scenes
and fight scenes.
Often there was music.

Will loved the theatre.
He loved the excitement of it.
He decided he wanted to be an actor.

Will soon got to know
some of the actors.
He became friends
with the famous actor, James Burbage.
He joined Burbage's company
and became an actor.
He was only given small parts
to play at first.

He also began to write plays
for Burbage's company.
His first play was called
The Comedy of Errors.
It was based on an old story,
but Will told it in his own way.
It is about two pairs of twins
who keep mixing each other up.
Perhaps having twins of his own
gave him the idea.

The play was a success.
Will carried on writing.

He became friends
with other playwrights.
He knew the playwright
Christopher Marlowe.
He was also good friends
with the famous playwright, Ben Jonson.
They used to drink,
talk and laugh together
in London's taverns.
A portrait of Will shows that he had
a high forehead, a beard,
brown eyes and a gold earring.

London was very lively at that time.
It was also very violent.
Ben Jonson once killed a man in a duel.
Christopher Marlowe was stabbed to death
in a fight in a tavern.

They were dangerous times.
And in 1592, they became
even more dangerous.

The Plague hit London.

4 The Plague

The Plague was also called
the Black Death.
It swept through England
every few years,
killing thousands.

It was carried by fleas
that lived on rats,
but nobody knew this.
Some people thought it was
God's punishment for their sins.

London was the perfect place
for the Plague to spread.
It was crowded, dirty
and full of rats.
Between 1592 and 1594,
ten thousand Londoners died
from the Plague.

Will was lucky enough
to escape the Plague.
But while it was raging,
the theatres closed down.
There was no point in writing plays.
He began to write poetry.
Some of his poems were published
and earned him money.

He also wrote over 150 sonnets.
A sonnet is a short poem of 14 lines.
Will didn't write these to be published.
They were personal poems –
love poems.
Some were written to a young man,
'Mr W. H.'
No one knows who he was.
Others were written to a 'Dark Lady'.
No one knows who she was, either.
The sonnets show very strong feelings
of love and jealousy.

In 1594, the Plague was over.
The theatres opened up again.
Will went back to writing plays.

We don't hear any more about Mr W. H.
or the Dark Lady.
But in his later plays,
Will often wrote about strong feelings
of love and jealousy.

5 Success

Will became London's
most successful playwright.
He wrote every kind of play.

He wrote tragedies
like *Romeo and Juliet*.

He wrote comedies
like *A Midsummer Night's Dream*.

He wrote history plays
like *Richard III*
and *Henry V*.

He was still an actor
in Burbage's company.
He often acted in his own plays.
As well as acting in the theatre,
the company put on plays at court
for Queen Elizabeth I.

Will bought shares in Burbage's company.
He became rich.
He bought shares
in London's new theatre, the Globe.
He bought a coat of arms for his father.
Will also bought land in Stratford.
He started to go back there more often
to see his family.

He bought the second biggest house
in Stratford, called New Place.
His wife and daughters lived there.
His son, Hamnet, died in 1596
when he was 11 years old.

This loss stayed with Will
for the rest of his life.
In his plays, he often wrote
of the pain of losing children.

In 1603, Queen Elizabeth died
and James I became King.
Will's company changed their name
to the King's Men.

Will was now at the height of his success.
He began to write his greatest plays.
They were tragedies,
full of strong feelings of love and jealousy,
cruelty and sadness.

His most famous tragedies are
Hamlet, Othello,
King Lear,
Antony and Cleopatra
and *Macbeth.*

6 Macbeth

Macbeth was written for James I,
who was Scottish.
It is one of Shakespeare's
most famous tragedies.

The story goes like this:
Macbeth was a Scottish Lord
and a soldier.
He was the bravest, toughest soldier
in the Scottish army.
At first he was loyal to Duncan,
the Scottish King.
He fought for Duncan against rebels
and beat them.

After the battle, he met three witches.
They told him that he would become
King of Scotland.
Macbeth was very ambitious.
He liked the idea of becoming King.
But he would have to
get rid of Duncan first.

He told his wife, Lady Macbeth, about it.
She liked the idea, too.
She told Macbeth
he would have to murder Duncan.

Soon after this, Duncan came to stay
at their castle.
Lady Macbeth made her husband
murder Duncan in the night.
Then she helped Macbeth
to cover up the murder.

Macbeth was made King.
Malcolm, Duncan's son,
escaped to England.

Now that Macbeth
had started murdering people,
he couldn't stop.
Anyone who got in his way
was killed.
He killed his friend Banquo,
because the witches had told him
that Banquo's sons would be kings.
Banquo's ghost returned to haunt him.

The witches also told him to fear
another soldier called Macduff.
Macduff joined Malcolm in England
and they raised an army.

Macbeth sent his men
to Macduff's castle.
They murdered Macduff's wife
and children.

Lady Macbeth, meanwhile,
went mad with guilt and died.

The army of Malcolm and Macduff
attacked Macbeth's army
and beat them.
Macduff killed Macbeth
in single combat.

In the last scene of the play,
Macduff comes onto the stage
with Macbeth's head on a pole.
Malcolm is made King of Scotland.

7 Last Years

Will's last play was called
The Tempest.
It is not a tragedy,
but a strange, magical play
about a shipwreck
and an enchanted island.

One of the main characters is a wizard.
At the end of the play,
he breaks his magic staff
and says he will do no more magic.
Some people think this was
Will saying goodbye to the theatre.

In 1610, Will returned to Stratford
to live.
He was not a young man any more.
He had had enough
of the excitement of London.
He wanted some peace and quiet.

Will died in 1616
on his birthday.
He was 52.
He left most of his money and property
to his eldest daughter, Susanna,
and her husband.
He left his wife his second-best bed.
No one knows why.

He is buried in the church
at Stratford.
On his grave are these words,
written by him:

'Good friend, for Jesus' sake forbear
To dig the dust enclosed here.
Blessed be the man
that spares these stones
And cursed be he
that moves my bones.'

8 Will's Words

Will wrote 37 plays in all
– tragedies, histories and comedies.
Not one was published
in his lifetime.

Seven years after his death,
two actor friends of his,
Heminges and Condell,
decided to publish them.
Since then, the plays
have become known
all over the world.
They are still put on
nearly 400 years after Will's death.

Will had a gift
for making up vivid phrases
that stick in the mind.
Many of them have become
part of the English language.

Here are a few of them:

- All's well that ends well
- Cruel to be kind
- I haven't slept a wink
- The winter of discontent
- At one fell swoop
- Love is blind
- The milk of human kindness
- In my mind's eye

You probably hear Shakespeare's words
every day without realising it.

Key Dates

23 April 1564   William Shakespeare
born at Stratford-upon-Avon

1582   Shakespeare marries
Ann Hathaway

1587   Goes to London
and becomes an actor

1591   Writes *The Comedy of Errors*

1592   The Black Death hits London.
Theatres close.
Shakespeare writes his sonnets
to 'Mr W. H.' and the 'Dark Lady'

1594   Theatres open again.
Shakespeare writes *Romeo and Juliet*

1596   Shakespeare's son Hamnet dies

1603   Elizabeth I dies.
James I becomes King.

1605   Shakespeare writes *Macbeth*

1610   Retires to Stratford

23 April 1616   Shakespeare dies

1624   Shakespeare's plays are published
in the First Folio edition